Apophenia

poems by

Jeremy Freedman

Finishing Line Press
Georgetown, Kentucky

Apophenia

Copyright © 2017 by Jeremy Freedman
ISBN 978-1-63534-378-6 First Edition
All rights reserved under International and Pan-American Copyright Conventions.
No part of this book may be reproduced in any manner whatsoever without written permission from the publisher, except in the case of brief quotations embodied in critical articles and reviews.

ACKNOWLEDGMENTS

Duck Duck Goose and Nothing and Something first appeared in *Alien Mouth*
A View of a Storm first appeared in *Eclectica Magazine*
The Venetian first appeared in *Message in a Bottle*
The Day After Lou Reed Died first appeared in *Cartagena Journal*
Exit Zero first appeared in *Otoliths*
Why We Can't Have Nice Things first appeared in *Queen Mob's Teahouse*
School of Fish first appeared in *Pioneertown*
Waffle House first appeared in *Wu Wei Fashion Mag*
Summer's Cold Air first appeared in *Orbis*
Millipede and Vir Heroicus Sublimus (for Frank O'Hara) first appeared in *The Missing Slate*

Publisher: Leah Maines

Editor: Christen Kincaid

Cover Art: Jeremy Freedman

Author Photo: Jeremy Freedman

Cover Design: Elizabeth Maines McCleavy

Printed in the USA on acid-free paper.
Order online: www.finishinglinepress.com
　　　　　also available on amazon.com

　　　　　　　　Author inquiries and mail orders:
　　　　　　　　　　Finishing Line Press
　　　　　　　　　　　P. O. Box 1626
　　　　　　　　　Georgetown, Kentucky 40324
　　　　　　　　　　　　U. S. A.

Table of Contents

Duck Duck Goose 1

A View of a Storm 2

Saying Your Name Sincerely 3

Kiss-Cam 5

The Ladder 7

Nostalgia in Tompkins Square 8

The Venetian 10

Robespierre 11

Modern Virgins, or, The Pietà 12

The Day After Lou Reed Died 13

Exit Zero 16

Why We Can't Have Nice Things 17

Nothing and Something 18

Bragadin 19

The Nature of Sleep 21

School of Fish 22

Your Dog Loves My Dog 23

The War of the Spanish Succession 24

Waffle House 25

Millipede 26

Octopus 27

The Ferocious Tenth 28

Against Forgetting 30

Craquelure 31

Summer's Cold Air 33

Vir Heroicus Sublimus (for Frank O'Hara) 34

Duck Duck Goose

I have several of Donald Duck's
most inauspicious traits:
I'm pretty but I'm boring,
I'm moodier than the usual,
my urine is a dull yellow,
my beak hangs unhinged
when I doff my hat,
I only wear underwear
on my birthday.
I'm jejune,
I'm willing to shill,
I butter my scones
with Sisyphus's groans,
my pupils don't dilate
when I shut the lights.

When I shut the lights
the years weigh heavy;
I carry them high,
thrust out in front.
I demand your seat
on the subway.
I'm up to my feet
in chicken soup.
My left breast is bigger
than my right—that's right
where my heart sits.

That's right where my heart sits,
hovering below the choir,
as big as the Higgs boson,
right above my distended stomach.
My lips taste like duck sauce:
surely this is my ducktail
I feel with my duckhand.

A View of a Storm

The day before the rain began,
another jazz martyr ascended,
carrying his crystal tenor,
and returned to water.
Maybe it was Albert Ayler, the Holy Ghost.

Then it rained forever
until the Hudson
burst its banks at
23rd Street and the East River
poured into Avenue C.
I saw it from my window:
the fishes, freed, walked on land.

When 14th Street exploded,
Manhattan cut in two.
With darkness like a
diminuendo descending,
wounded starlings fell from the sky,
littering the ground
from Breezy Point to Hell Gate,
but still unfilled
the empty spaces are unfilled.

Saying Your Name Sincerely

I want to say your name
has a certain iridescence
like mother of pearl
and pearl coincidentally
was my mother's middle name
but first I want to bore myself
with your name if I may
I want to try to say it sincerely
over and over again
use it like a drug all day
so it wakes me in the morning
and knocks me out at night
I want to pop your name
in my mouth like an all-purpose
time-release medication
and feel it on my tongue
like a tumor
until it either dissolves
into pathetic fallacy
or hardens into rumor
of happiness
I know I sound sincere
when I say your name
to your ear my sincerity
appears to be sincere
to me my sincerity feels
almost not quite audible
someone is calling your name
from inside the house
like in a film
I'm home alone
I'm calling for myself alone
self-pity is a wily vice

like self-abuse or one
too many cocktails
you may say
get out of the house
when I say your name
but only when I say
your name sincerely
do I hear your voice

Kiss-Cam

I had my first kiss ever
on the kiss-cam
at old Yankee Stadium
and it was delish
I am what I am
sayeth the lord
I saw you eat
a hot dog with relish
and yellow mustard
I saw what seemed to be
a beatific human face
Soyuz over the bleachers
and cover the averages
and out of town scores
and advertising hoardings
on the Jumbotron
of the House That Ruth Built
eclipsing the scary truth
that I'm the apopheniacal
scion of my own
fan fiction history
I was weeping freshets
when the game ended
in a rain delay

I'm only as goodish
as I have to be
just like the ninety-nine
percent of freaks
who undervalue romance
in favor of kitsch
they think they're
owning it
they think their store-bought

friends will stay bought
they think they roll
their own New York City
maybe I lied about that kiss
and it wasn't that good
maybe it was kind of shitty

The Ladder

Most suffering
is lost to history;
it's too good
to be remembered.
Because the ladder
is always wobbly,
there is always hope
that someone might fall,
one imagines happily.
Imagination is the chaste
privilege of the living.
I like to imagine how,
when someone dies,
there will be one thing
less to think about:
for instance, an age,
a preoccupation,
a friendship,
a desire,
a career,
a disease,
how wet one gets
crossing the river in
the ruinous pursuit of art,
the insufferable popularity
of some pop star
who turns out to be
smarter than me,
and who understands
why death
is nothing personal.

Nostalgia in Tompkins Square

elevated in an émigré fog
I saw your atemporal ghost
walking down St. Marks Place
hand in hand with yourself
and the hairy itinerants and the Fugs
and a lapsed Egyptian elf
with no flex in his pecs
and the mohawked imps
honest I've got the pics
they incriminate only me
but I'm not confessing
you carried your random
non-denominational passport
off-handedly in your dirty paw
I don't have to be right
but I know what I saw
crawl before you walk
walk before you fall
in an affected heap
on the spittled sidewalk
in front of the Gem Spa
and follow me to the greasy
excremented cement
of Tompkins Square
make a list
of what the comics carry
lie down there on Avenue A
when your burden gets too heavy
it was so long since we played
thirsty camel in the desert
I thought I wasn't going to make it
my face was razed
my body was racked
but this is not a confession
the monk's heads were shaved
and their saffron robes have turned
hot pink in the whipsawed light
of the Dom I felt it was inevitable
when someone let the dog bark

all through the exploding
snowy x-massy night
you could hear it bark
all the way to Hoboken
where we went to cop an eight ball
and then hoovered it up
on the taxi-ride home
all weekend on the couch
with a carton of Luckies
and a bottle of bourbon
then five minutes in heaven
you touched my face
and took off your shirt
it was the best you could do
of course it wasn't anything
I hadn't seen before
like that time you flashed me
in the car on I-95 on the way
to New Haven for a lecture
at the School of Divinity
on the stained glass of Chartres
I loved your tits I swear
they're America's smallest
and most charming even
if they were a little uneven
I licked them like the starving
once licked stamps for nourishment
they remind me how a composition
can remain unfinished
and still be alarming
brutally dissonant and beautiful
that's still not a confession
merely an opinion I hope
it reaches you
the opposite may also be true

The Venetian

I traveled to you by air, by land, by water:
the air viscid as honey with expectation,
the land covered to depth with the dust of dreams,
the water that brought us together and kept us apart.
We are separated by hundreds of years
and the sinister habits of Europe,
separated by the distance
from Vilna to Venice,
from ghetto to palazzo,
from my grandfather's grandfather,
who saw Napoleon's army, defeated and dying and returning to France,
to yours, who welcomed the hero of Italy.
In the *traghetto*, the oarsman told me to sit down,
but you are permitted to stand.
My dream is of you, Venice -
you're as thin as paper,
as serious as happiness, take care!

Robespierre

What part of the sky
is the bluest blue?
Closer to the horizon
or in the other direction?
Perhaps it depends
on the way you're walking,
with head up or down,
or, on the last day of November,
there might not be any blue at all.
It's easy to see
from here to the river
in the east, the river
the color of November.
From here to the river, the city
is laid out like Robespierre
on the scaffold, face-up
with his neck beneath
the blade, the city,
like a Jacobin,
crying out with
its flattened vowels,
slogans of revolution
until the last breath,
its voice as frayed
as the night's last siren
as it passed 23rd and First
on the way perhaps to Bellevue
carrying precious cargo,
reversing Robespierre's route
in his tumbrel, as he rolled
to the place of execution,
silenced, his jaw shattered,
wounded and unable to stand,
his eyes fixed on the bluest
part of the Thermidor sky.

Modern Virgins, or, The Pietà

Only snobs want to get hammered
with the Virgin Mary
in the VIP section
of Club Miserere.
She's a tough old broad,
tough as nails,
flesh as hard as diamonds,
and her beating heart
can really hold her liquor.
But when she's loaded
and feeling shitty,
she gets a little cross
and swears an oath to pity.

Meanwhile, at closing time, her wayward
son is just showing up. He's so flash.
On her word, he drove the snakes
from the temple with his rod
and staff, and bit the head off the worm
like a geek. He breached the thorny wall
of decorum with his antics, sloughed
off the chain-mail armor of his robes
and removed the thorny helmet
of his self-sacrificing semantics.

Nobody's perfect, he's come to learn:
he's suffering a temporary paralysis.
He has a holy-week hangover
and an ugly rash and he's flummoxed
about the scars of the confessional.
His body is a mystery, even to him.
He needs to purge with hyssop
and cool his head in a gallon of froyo
before he gorks.

The Day After Lou Reed Died

1.
The day after Lou Reed died I had a colonoscopy,
so I would have thought about mortality
anyway, if not mine then someone else's,
maybe someone I really knew.

I thought of Steven Wayne, a former pal who
shot himself for the shock value.
His bequest enabled his survivors
to build a house of straw on the Connecticut River
and go careening, none too gently, ass over teakettle.

I thought of many-dimpled Sarah Rattle
whose frequent lapses and resurrections and battles
entranced and enchanted but ultimately ended
with a dose of mercury and blood,
a mesmeric scene worthy of the end of Harold
as shown on the Bayeux Tapestry,
the World War Z of its day.

And I thought of my father, lying in a dissection tray,
who finally couldn't hold his breath or get his way.
They bisected his brain by the shining
big sea water (this is no myth, Hiawatha).
Nothing to choose between
Lucia's mad scene and John the Revelator,
until finally, in the midnight hour,
his love came tumbling down,
and he provided for all those little Attilas
who then sacked and plundered his bounty
and left a shuddering trail of loss flooding
from town to city and county to county.

2.
So anyway, back to me and my colonoscopy:
They scoped me up and down and sideways,
they practically fracked me,
searching for the conqueror worm.
They labored over me
as if I were giving birth
to the urgent oyster of Bethlehem
or some monstrous blob of something,
Rosemary's baby, maybe.
They looked and looked,
even Madame Sosostris looked,
icy speculum in hand, eyes as old
as the last century is old,
her bad cold and all, looking
for evidence of disaster,
but she didn't know the useful question
so she didn't get a useful answer.

3.
Then Lou Reed entered
through the usual way
and delivered of me this poem.
I hadn't felt this bad about the death
of an artist I didn't know, since I don't know,
since Sebald ran his car off the road
(how could he be so stupid?).

But VU videos on YouTube helped me fill
the blue grotto of public sadness for Lou.
It was the least I could do. After all,
his faith and works at the siege
of Constantinople nearly carried the day.

I played Femme Fatale and Sister Ray
until I started to smile, and even after
the Venetians carried the four horses
back to San Marco, his nasal voice represented
to me my private grief for my own departed,
and departed strangers, though unknown to me;
it was then I had the happy reverie to play
the home movies of other families.

These are not my memories I play but they are
like my memories of fuzzy, puzzled love.
I play the living who no longer live,
I put them through their fatal paces
and they give and give from beyond the grave.
Whatever else they have to give,
they give the answers that I crave.

Exit Zero

1.
The wind is blowing
the paper along the highway;
it rolls past exit zero
where the living birds fly
in both directions.

Below the divide
the wind is blowing hard
that's all anyone can talk about.

I see skin mottled like handmade paper
picked over by snag-toothed mammals
until it bleeds purple.
That's what I talk about.

2.
At exit zero
I dreamed of hazy ceremonies,
I dreamed stilts replaced my legs,
I dreamed Courbet's stags were freed
and Medusa's raft triangulated
above the water.

3.
At exit zero
Life meaning life is the sentence;
we think the world
long-limbed and feverish,
plaited with desire, as a house
seen at night from the lawn,
filled with fireflies, each fly-light equal,
flashing in all directions.

Why We Can't Have Nice Things

When a man loves a woman
and winces with discomfort,
when a worm wins a ribbon
for skydiving like a baby airplane
that's lost its way instead
of doing something useful
like learning to dance the tango
or read Rilke in the original
I'm gonna say German,
these velleities (to use an
Ashbery word) are not consonant
(to use another) with one's life
as lived and never will be,
one's paralogy will not allow for it.
How subtle one is one thinks
to turn the misery of adventure
into a naissance of ordinary
unhappiness, one's thumbprints
barely visible on the pages
of the abandoned autobiography.

Nothing and Something

It's been a week
since I ran out of milk;
that's the sum total
of all that's happened
since I came home from Italy,
where I saw the tenderest
Bellini mother and child
in the Brera,
and also saw there
in the faces of men
in the shadows of the sunset
at the Disputation's edge
how solitude can be performed
in plain view.
It's easy to write about nothing:
nothing is what we know
when the day is foggy
and the apartment
has no heat
and no trip to Italy,
no matter how recent,
can compensate.
Not so easy to write
about something:
the mortadella
I smuggled home,
hidden in my carry-on,
just so
I had some skin
in the game
and when hungry
another creature's
viscera
to pick at.

Bragadin

It's surprisingly easy to find
the Facebook page
of Marcantonio Bragadin,
Venetian commander of Cyprus,
flayed alive in Famagusta
for God and St. Mark in 1571.
Pictures posted prove
he's living it up baller style
in the Venetian hotel in Las Vegas.
That's his reward for bravely
bearing his abandonment to the enemy
and how savagely he was used.

Now he's living with verve,
in Vegas, the pictures show.
He's hired as a helper,
a parasympathetic nurse
to supply supple transverse
stimulation to his vagus nerve.

Thanks to tincture of storax,
he's recovered use of his larynx,
so now he can relax
and engage full-throatedly
in intercourse of every sort,
even with the mighty Turks.

He's refilled his thorax
with heart and lungs.
He can bend again at the waist
after all this time and hear and see
again and he's just about
to start training for a UFC
undercard heavyweight bout.

He's as busy as Cinderfella
praying and moaning for his sins,
while dressing for the ball
and dropping the broom.
He's juggling his weight loss,
his falsetto's teeth are in
he's ready to face up
and lower the boom.
He's comfortable in his new skin.

The Nature of Sleep

outside it's dark as chaste Diana's sin
we choose to retire
on your normal bridal schedule
and prepare ourselves accordingly
shedding our skin
for the common vulnerability
what can go wrong while we're asleep?
that we will forget how
it feels to be awake?
that we will believe our dreams?
that our words will regain
their original meanings
as if it's not enough to remember?
perhaps only in sleep will we begin
to think clearly and the stress
on our hearts will be relieved
you choose what bed we use
your temperature falls
your breathing slows
but no matter how long we lie here
your hands and feet remain
cold to the touch
your body predicts the future

School of Fish

I am not a alone. Instead of people,
I saw a listing school of fish
fisting from side to side,
and their desires;
they were on drugs.
I ate tree bark and beetles and bugs
and the sea knew me.
I was almost convinced
I was almost a merman, but I knew
it wasn't true because I couldn't tell
my left-hand flipper what to do.
I paid strangers to watch me
eat myself; I'm the last doughnut
in a box of doughnuts.

Your Dog Loves My Dog

I see that your dog loves my dog.
Recline with me by the roots
of the apple tree
in the garden and we shall see
what side of time's gnome you're on.
We shall see if you are.

I see how your dog loves my dog.
Perhaps your dog could read me
this poem, and maybe one other,
enunciating in its poshest accent,
pronouncing as clearly as it can.

And then I shall be the disciple of your dog:
I shall have no other dogs before me.
All I will know is what your dog tells me:
How you will love me like a dog
loves another dog, more than I can bear,
beyond what even dogs can hear.

The War of the Spanish Succession

Two negronis and a white russian
walk into a bar together
which is the last thing
anyone ever expected,
even as a joke,
given the cultural difficulties.
Usually it's the other way around,
as the shy pornographer said,
carnalizing the third of May.
Corpse used to mean body
now it means dead body,
and all the bloodshed that entails.
The entrails of the infanta are hung
with great care from the balusters
of the palace like Christmas stockings.
The last remaining servant
carefully sweeps the *idée fixe*
of the old regime from the balcony
while anarchists in the antechamber
demonstrate the proper way
to make milk toast
and gum their way to irrelevance.
They're unbelievabled again,
they don't think perfection is possible,
but at least they remember their dreams.

Waffle House

every scene
at the Waffle House
is a crime scene
every body is lying
in a pool of butter
they don't know
how they got here
they just don't remember
when they reached
a fork in the road
to this jurisdiction
on a journey
to being a girl
with the Domesday Book
on her reading list
it's so horrible
I want to live here
forever
in fear
of my nature
that nature
plagiarizes
every chaos
is compelling
the future
will ruin my life
if it can penetrate
my soggy sopping brain
if the information
means anything
it's always
fat Tuesday

Millipede

For a thousand years,
I haven't wanted to remember
how good it felt to be debased,
but now I want to return,
return to that alerted night,
when you walked on my face
with a thousand legs like a millipede,
as if you owned the place.

Something clarified in me
that fragrant night,
my blood as thick as butter,
and every hair on my body
stood up to welcome you,
and make a nest
for the thousand tiny eggs
you chose to lay.

By the next morning,
your exquisite eggs had fabergéd
into hatchlings I'd have to raise
alone, because you were gone,
like the moment was,
as if you'd never been.

I know you're out there though,
skittering across someone's face
on your thousand skinny legs,
and I know I'll have to swim
a filthy river
just to lick your nutmeg
skin again and taste
how you taste, of mace.

Octopus

I think of your friend the octopus,
sitting tamely on your thigh.
He remembers everything he's learned
about mathematics and physics,
philosophy and politics,
and he's happy to tell you.

I've heard that the octopus is intelligent
and has three hearts, all carefully attuned
to your desires, and I remember how he used
his eight tensile arms to build the world's
most beautiful monuments, including:

- Palazzo Ducale
- Colossus of Rhodes
- Pharos of Alexandria
- Alhambra
- Taj Mahal

And I've even heard the story
of how he propelled himself upward
by the strength of his suctioned arms
from the depths of the sea to the top
of the Hanging Gardens of Babylon,
and from there into your lap.
And once there, he used his beak
to break the fabric of the world.

Who, if anyone, is hurt by that?
Only those below, on the ground,
outside the embrace of eight powerful
arms, staring with mouths agape
like naïve, startled tourists.

The Ferocious Tenth

There is a popular future,
even in this life, I'm convinced,
that's as tantalizingly close
and impractical and hunkered down
as bloody charlotte russe,
or poor obsolete peaches melba,
too passé to survive,
or, like uncertain baked Alaska,
unadapted to current conditions,
half unfrozen and melting
masochistically on the plate.

Unadapted enough though one is,
to breast stroke like the unconditional
poet, who swam the Hellespont
and icy Bering Strait, eyes drama'd shut,
buoyed by water wings
and inflated imaginings,
and later crossed the Lagoon
from Molo to Lido, past San Lazzaro,
though that's a roundabout
way to compensate
for boundaries and defects
one is doomed to beat
one's uncrowned head
and limping feet against.
His heavenly quest for celebrity's
boundless and limpid effects
foundered on the same slippery
rock, the very foundation,
we all stand upon, half
in water and half on dry land.

If you can stand to hear,
I'd like you to listen
to the ferocious Tenth
Transcendental Etude of Liszt,
marked *Allegro agitato molto.*
In truth, every work of Liszt
is ferocious and glistens
in its own super-emotional way,
that's what makes them romantic,
but the Tenth really rocks.
It fills your ears like rush hour
or the crush on a jetway.

It's an instrument as useful
as a machine for drawing
water from wells we had thought
were dry, and for resolving
every complication that follows.
In its attack on the theory
of liberty that killed the poet
almost as soon as he was taught
it, we see an inspiration only as clear
as the shallow, murky Lagoon,
or, like the water in a water balloon,
falsely and insufficiently transparent.

Against Forgetting

If it makes the superstitious more comfortable
to imagine the open wounds are closed,
then let them imagine. Because one
coldcock deserves another.

With a low wink, the Chinese character
for fuck suddenly appears on my chest.
Why not? Everything seeks its own level.
And it's Jimmy Week again.

You've been waiting for him; invite him in
for a glass of your worst pinot noir.
He wants to tripe your shorts
and he's ready to preach to the choir.

I'm death's guilty pleasure,
a treasureless character lost
in the Moritat of Mackie Messer,
the master-wolf of no regret.

Muskrats will shake my ass;
so says Hanging Judge Fogarty.
It's a fait accompli, he says, should have
shown trumps and offered cash.

Since the days of the dinosaurs
and Titus sacked the Temple
and Apollinaire was born in a nail factory
in Poland, already dressed in black,

And Bogart, coughing, put down his last Lucky Strike,
and up until now, I've forgotten nothing.
So wake up the dead and step out of the shade,
this is the world we must have made.

Craquelure

I remember my amnesia. How it was torture
to love the low-country crab, so spiny.

I remember how my clothes had no texture,
the wale as smooth as ivory.

I remember your dainty embouchure,
the aperture through which you blew.

You made the sign of the fleur
de lis over my hot pastrami

and before I could blink I was a goner
and my food had no flavor.

I was a novitiate in aspirature,
bawling my balled-up American vowels.

You took my poisoned verdigris nature
by storm, and my buzzing blood apprehended

just one voice in the numbrous choir
playing judge the world: yours.

Attracted by my craquelure,
the lacquered surface drying with detachment,

the need for healing moisture
rising eagerly, apparent at a glance,

you undertook the cure d'amour,
the work of conservation.

You foster-cared my furniture,
the crib and rocker of my obsolescence.

So soft the bravura fur you wore,
all fox-heads, tails and paws,

as you waxed and polished the tonsure,
the surface brought to a sheen,

with spit and salt water you were juror
and executioner inserting the needle.

But you gave yourself leave to usure
and raised my interest rate too high,

and you put me under pressure,
like the dog who chased the car

at a hundred miles an hour
and finally caught it by the tire.

If I were safe in a sinecure,
a footnote to a footnote,

or if I became a dog of leisure,
then I'd bite the tire to test it,

and I'd lick the tire's puncture
around its acid edge

and straighten out my posture
only when I'm put to rest

in someone else's sepulcher,
drugged as a bug in a rug.

Summer's Cold Air

Traveling from disbelieving
disarray to uncertain despair
to sure knowledge of failure,
happy to share coincidence,
I circled your name in a magazine.
Or a name something like your name.

I thought of us by the statue
of Colleoni at San Zanipolo,
where the families of *Il Libro d'Oro*
honored their captain-general,
but also wronged him:
they betrayed their condescension.

We circled the monument;
the cold air kept us awake.
As we walked I thanked you
for bringing the coldness of your glamor
into my life, and a feeling of strangeness.
Your mouth is filled with rose petals,
your hands with the softest down.
Your body is a sponge, absorbing
the waters of history.

Vir Heroicus Sublimus (for Frank O'Hara)

In July 1966,
weeping and wailing was heard
from Cherry Grove to Corneille Estates,
even to Louse Point and Montauk,
and all the way to Shelter Island.
No taxis cruised, no paint was placed or flung
and St. Marks Place was paralyzed with grief.

"Subject matter is never a problem.
Words are like a field of wheat; my job
is to turn the wheat into bread.
Bakers are the opposite of
heroic but somehow sublime.

This work is not an expression
of mundane habit, I am
avoiding the void, depicting
the excitement of living,
bringing us to the abyss.

But I am involved in human life too
and I think, Barney, we should go
and have a drink right now -
and then no more dying!"

Jeremy Freedman is a writer and artist living in New York City. His previous careers include video editor and attorney. His poems have been published in numerous journals and his photographs have been exhibited in the United States and abroad.

He likes chips with salsa and/or guacamole but the guacamole must be made in a specific way or he will be disappointed. He may express his disappointment loudly and with rancor or he may just sulk.

His current favorite alcoholic drink is a dirty martini but without vermouth so not really a martini and on the rocks. He tries to limit his alcohol intake for health reasons and is sometimes successful.

The fate of the world is in his hands. He wonders just a little whether all these words bring the end closer to the beginning or vice versa. He prefers if possible to avoid awkward social interactions. He has recently revised his opinion about certain well-regarded twentieth century artists. His thoughts swarm like fire ants. He navigates underground streams by dead reckoning. He mines gold from the bedrock of Manhattan and silver tears from your eyes.

www.ingramcontent.com/pod-product-compliance
Lightning Source LLC
LaVergne TN
LVHW041559070426
835507LV00011B/1197